Editor
Dona Herweck Rice

Editor-in-Chief
Sharon Coan, M.S. Ed.

Illustrator
Blanca Apodaca

Cover Artist
Barb Lorseyedi

Art Coordinator
Kevin Barnes

Imaging
Alfred Lau
James Edward Grace
Temo Parra

Product Manager
Phil Garcia

Publishers
Rachelle Cracchiolo, M.S. Ed.
Mary Dupuy Smith, M.S. Ed.

Year-Round Nonfiction
Mini Books

Author

Jan Burda

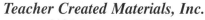

Teacher Created Materials, Inc.
6421 Industry Way
Westminster, CA 92683
www.teachercreated.com
ISBN-0-7439-3640-X
©2002 Teacher Created Materials, Inc.
Made in U.S.A.

Table of Contents

Definition and Uses

A *nonfiction mini book* is a small booklet consisting of pertinent or interesting facts about a certain topic. To make such a mini book, a standard-sized paper is divided into halves, thirds, or fourths to create the pages. The mini book is then photocopied by an adult and put together in sequence according to page numbers (which the students may be able to do, depending on their skill level). Usually pictures accompany the script on each page, but sometimes there is a space for students to draw the illustrations themselves. For the early learner (preschool through first grade) a sentence on each page is often enough.

In this resource book, two nonfiction topics have been selected for each month of the year (to accommodate year-round and traditional school years alike). However, the topics can be used anytime throughout the year. Also, a bibliography of nonfiction books has been included to accompany the mini books. The mini books here have been written for various purposes. Here are just a few of their uses:

- to increase sight vocabulary in the early learner

- to improve number comprehension and writing

- to teach color, shape, and number words

- to develop an understanding of the basic parts of a book (title, beginning, middle, end)

- to develop an understanding of what authors and illustrators do

- to expand each student's own book collection

- to develop a higher level of reading and comprehension for each student

- to supplement existing curriculum

Another unique feature of the mini books in this collection is that each one was written to correspond with a traditional song or chant, allowing the students a chance to sing or recite these books in a fun and engaging way. Studies show that singing and poetry can enhance student learning by increasing memory skills.

To further enhance memory, it is recommended that the teacher make sentence strips for each page from the mini book she or he has chosen to use. The sentence strips are put in a pocket chart along with the matching mini book page. The entire class can recite the book together, repeating the sentences several times and then singing the lines. Eventually, individual copies can be given to all students to color or illustrate themselves. Depending on the students' ages and the time available, the students can cut apart the pages and put them in order themselves. The mini books are then stored in the classroom and eventually sent home.

Assembly and Storage

The pages for all mini books can be copied and cut apart on the page lines, correlated, and stapled together in booklet form. (See the illustration below.)

Cut apart on lines.

Staple.

The teacher, a classroom aide, or a parent helper can prepare the mini books for the students. In some cases, the students can cut apart the pages, sequence them according to page numbers, and staple the booklets together themselves. This can be done at a center table or in a small group with an adult helper.

After the books have been assembled, the students can illustrate them and fill in any missing words, as necessary, and practice reading the books to one another.

Inexpensive storage for these mini books can be made from individual shoe or cereal boxes. Every student should have his or her own box. When using a cereal box, it is best to cut the box in half. Contact paper could be placed over the box to make it more attractive, but this is not necessary. On the shoebox end or cereal-box side panel, the student's name should be printed. The student's photograph should be glued or taped underneath his or her name, adding a personal touch to the storage box and making it easy for the student to find his or her own box quickly. All boxes should be placed on a bookshelf, in student cubbies, or on a low countertop so the students can reach them with ease. Putting them in alphabetical order is also helpful.

As the students finish their mini books, they can store them in their individual boxes. During free time, the students can get their boxes and reread their own mini books. Periodically, after several have been made, the books should be sent home with the students to create a mini-book library of their very own. Page 6 includes a special parent note that can be sent home, explaining how to use these mini books.

Extensions

Here are a variety of extensions for the twenty-four mini books included in this book.

- The teacher can prepare a mini-book center in the classroom at which students assemble and create teacher-made as well as their own mini books.

- Little buddies can read their own collection of mini books to their big buddies. Big buddies can help make mini books for their little buddies' collections.

- The mini books can be used as an introduction for a new unit of study.

- The mini books can be used for free-time reading.

- The mini books can be sent home periodically in an envelope or folder for the students to save and read to family members.

- The mini books can be used as homework assignments and sticker rewards can be given when each reading assignment is complete.

- When photocopied, the illustrations in the mini books can be deleted, allowing room for the students to illustrate the books themselves.

Parent Note

The following letter should be glued to a folder or envelope that contains each student's mini books.

Dear Parents,

Enclosed in this packet are special mini books that your child has put together here at school. The books contain repetitive language, rhymes, and pictures that help the children remember the words. It is suggested that your child often reread these mini books aloud to you or another family member. He or she should also be encouraged to read them on his or her own.

Throughout the year, a new mini book will be created on a weekly basis and sent home. The topics of these books are usually the same as the units we have been studying in the classroom. Please save these booklets in this folder and encourage your child to reread them several times a week.

Thank you for your help! These simple and engaging mini books will help your child learn to read. I hope you and your child enjoy these books.

Sincerely,

_____

1

Whales

(tune: "Did You Ever See a Lassie?")

This book belongs to:

_____

2

Did you ever see a blue whale, a blue whale, a blue whale?

Did you ever see a blue whale, 100 feet long?

3

Did you ever see an orca, an orca, an orca?

Did you ever see an orca hunting for seals?

4

Did you ever see a sperm whale, a sperm whale, a sperm whale?

Did you ever see a sperm whale spouting water in the air?

5

Did you ever hear a humpback, a humpback, a humpback?

Did you ever hear a humpback singing his song?

6

Did you ever see a gray whale, a gray whale, a gray whale?

Did you ever see a gray whale fluking her tail?

My Tide Pool Friends

(tune: "My Bonnie Lies Over the Ocean")

This book belongs to:

_____

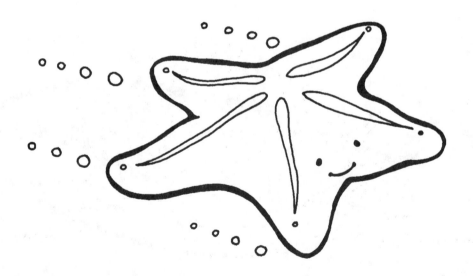

My starfish lives in a tide pool.

My starfish lives in the sea.

My starfish lives in a tide pool.

Oh, swim, my starfish, by me.

3

My octopus lives in a tide pool.

My octopus lives in the sea.

My octopus lives in a tide pool.

Oh, swim, my octopus, by me.

4

My sea urchin lives in a tide pool.

My sea urchin lives in the sea.

My sea urchin lives in a tide pool.

Oh, swim, my sea urchin, by me.

5

My crab lives in a tide pool.

My crab lives in the sea.

My crab lives in a tide pool.

Oh, swim, my crab, by me.

6

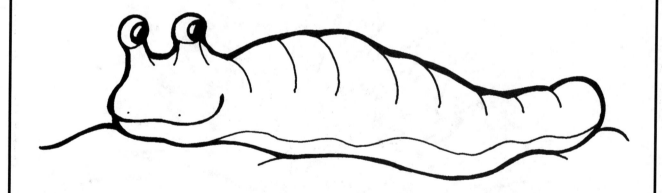

My sea slug lives in a tide pool.

My sea slug lives in the sea.

My sea slug lives in a tide pool.

Oh, swim, my sea slug, by me.

1

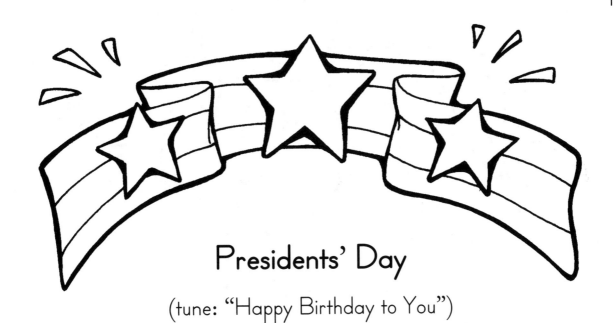

Presidents' Day

(tune: "Happy Birthday to You")

This book belongs to:

_____

2

Happy birthday, Abraham Lincoln,

Happy birthday to you!

You saved our country, Mr. Lincoln,

And freed the slaves, too!

3

Happy Birthday, George Washington,

Happy Birthday to you!

You were a general who saved our country,

And the first president, too!

4

Draw a picture of a birthday cake here. The cake is for Abraham Lincoln and George Washington.

Here is a special birthday cake for Abraham Lincoln and George Washington. I drew it myself. Happy birthday, Presidents!

Ten Little Candy Hearts

(tune: "Ten Little Indians")

This book belongs to:

_____

1

|||

One little . . .

2

2 2 2

Two little . . .

3

3 3 3

Three little candy hearts.

4

5

4 4 4

Four little . . .

6

5 5 5

Five little . . .

7

6 6 6

Six little candy hearts.

8

7 7 7

Seven little . . .

9

8 8 8

Eight little . . .

10

q q q

Nine little candy hearts.

11

10 10 10

Ten little candy hearts for you!

12

Ten little,
Nine little,
Eight little candy hearts,
Seven little,
Six little,
Five little candy hearts,
Four little,
Three little,
Two little candy hearts,
One little candy heart
left to chew!

1

Away We Go

(tune: "The Wheels on the Bus")

This book belongs to:

_____

2

First we traveled by walking on foot,

Walking on foot, walking on foot.

First we traveled by walking on foot all around the town.

3

Then we rode horses and carts,

Horses and carts, horses and carts.

Then we rode horses and carts all around the town.

4

Next we rode our bicycles,

Our bicycles, our bicycles.

Next we rode our bicycles all around the town.

5

Then we drove our cars and trucks,

Our cars and trucks, our cars and trucks.

Then we drove our cars and trucks all around the town.

6

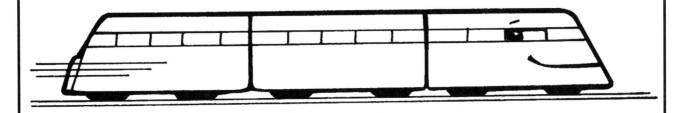

Next we rode in passenger trains,

Passenger trains, passenger trains.

Next we rode in passenger trains all around the town.

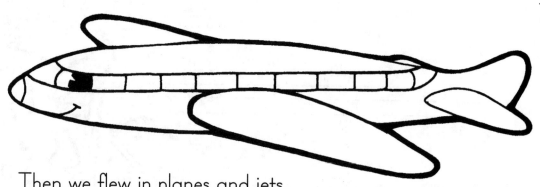

7

Then we flew in planes and jets,

Planes and jets, planes and jets.

Then we flew in planes and jets all around the town.

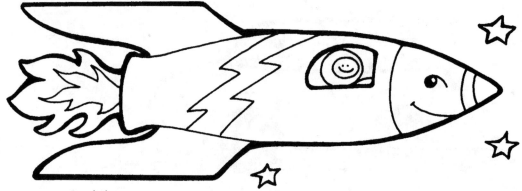

8

Now we travel in our spaceships,

Our spaceships, our spaceships.

Now we travel in our spaceships into outer space.

9

My favorite way to travel is by _____.

Here is a picture of my favorite transportation.

1

Dinosaurs, Dinosaurs

(tune: "Twinkle, Twinkle Little Star")

This book belongs to:

_____

2

Dinosaurs, dinosaurs, where are you?

Did you starve or get the flu?

3

What happened to the great beasts?

Did you become a T–Rex feast?

4

Dinosaurs, dinosaurs, we looked everywhere.

Maybe an earthquake gave you a scare!

5

Did the air just get too cold,

And then you died before you were old?

6

Dinosaurs, dinosaurs, where are you?

We put your fossil bones together with glue.

Dinosaurs, dinosaurs, I'm trying to think,

What ever happened to make you extinct?

1

Ten Little Eggs

(tune: "Here We Go 'Round the Mulberry Bush")

This book belongs to:

_____

2

Out of egg 1 comes a dinosaur,

A dinosaur, a dinosaur.

Out of egg 1 comes a dinosaur

So early in the morning.

3

Out of egg 2 comes a little lizard,

A little lizard, a little lizard.

Out of egg 2 comes a little lizard

So early in the morning.

4

Out of egg 3 comes a baby robin,

A baby robin, a baby robin.

Out of egg 3 comes a baby robin

So early in the morning.

5

444

Out of egg 4 comes a hummingbird,
A hummingbird, a hummingbird.
Out of egg 4 comes a hummingbird
So early in the morning.

6

555

Out of egg 5 comes a yellow duck,
A yellow duck, a yellow duck.
Out of egg 5 comes a yellow duck
So early in the morning.

7

666

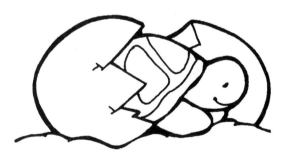

Out of egg 6 comes a green turtle,
A green turtle, a green turtle.
Out of egg 6 comes a green turtle
So early in the morning.

8

777

Out of egg 7 comes a slinky snake,
A slinky snake, a slinky snake.
Out of egg 7 comes a slinky snake
So early in the morning.

8 8 8   9

Out of egg 8 comes a tiny fish,

A tiny fish, a tiny fish.

Out of egg 8 comes a tiny fish

So early in the morning.

9 9 9   10

Out of egg 9 comes a happy spider,

A happy spider, a happy spider.

Out of egg 9 comes a happy spider

So early in the morning.

10 10 10   11

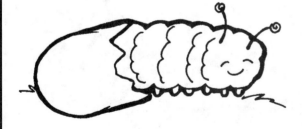

Out of egg 10 comes a caterpillar,

A caterpillar, a caterpillar.

Out of egg 10 comes a caterpillar

So early in the morning.

12

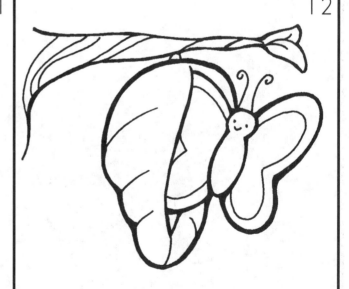

The caterpillar builds a cocoon,

Builds a cocoon, builds a cocoon.

The caterpillar builds a cocoon

And soon is a butterfly!

1

Springtime

(tune: "Mary Had a Little Lamb")

This book belongs to:

_____

2

Springtime always smells so good, smells so good, smells so good.

Springtime always smells so good, everywhere I go.

3

Springtime means the sun shines more, sun shines more, sun shines more.
Springtime means the sun shines more, everywhere I go.

4

Springtime brings baby animals, baby animals, baby animals.
Springtime brings baby animals, everywhere I go.

5

Springtime is a time for growth, time for growth, time for growth.

Springtime is a time for growth, everywhere I go.

6

Now, draw a picture of yourself in the spring.

Springtime is the time for me, time for me, time for me.

Springtime is the time for me, everywhere I go.

The Life of a Butterfly

(tune: "The Farmer in the Dell")

This book belongs to:

_____

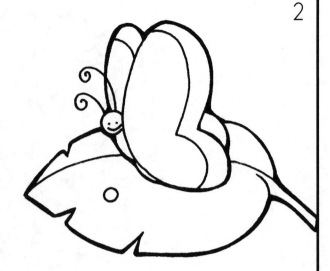

2

The butterfly lays an egg.

The butterfly lays an egg.

This is the life of a butterfly.

The butterfly lays an egg.

3

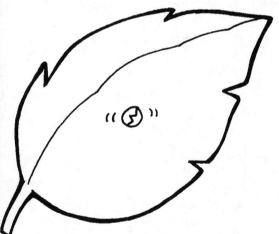

The egg hatches open.

The egg hatches open.

This is the life of a butterfly.

The egg hatches open.

4

A caterpillar crawls out.

A caterpillar crawls out.

This is the life of a butterfly.

A caterpillar crawls out.

5

The caterpillar eats and eats.

The caterpillar eats and eats.

This is the life of a butterfly.

The caterpillar eats and eats.

6

The caterpillar grows and grows.

The caterpillar grows and grows.

This is the life of a butterfly.

The caterpillar grows and grows.

7

The caterpillar spins a cocoon.

The caterpillar spins a cocoon.

This is the life of a butterfly.

The caterpillar spins a cocoon.

8

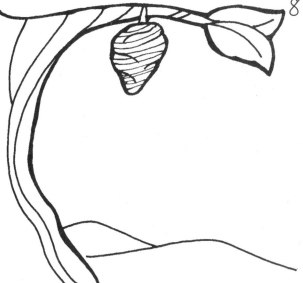

The cocoon hangs on the branch.

The cocoon hangs on the branch.

This is the life of a butterfly.

The cocoon hangs on the branch.

9

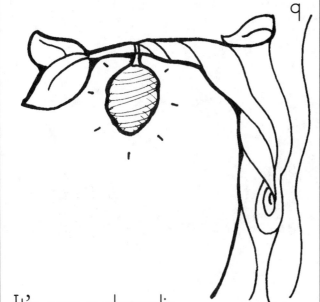

It's now a chrysalis.

It's now a chrysalis.

This is the life of a butterfly.

It's now a chrysalis.

10

Days

It waits for fourteen days.

It waits for fourteen days.

This is the life of a butterfly.

It waits for fourteen days.

11

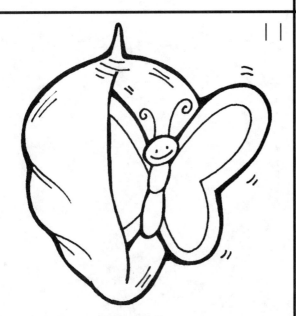

Out comes a butterfly.

Out comes a butterfly.

This is the life of a butterfly.

Out comes a butterfly.

12

And now it waves goodbye.

And now it waves goodbye.

This is the life of a butterfly.

And now it waves goodbye.

1

Itsy Bitsy Spider

(tune: "The Itsy Bitsy Spider")

This book belongs to:

_____

2

The itsy bitsy spider climbed up the web so high.

3

On the sticky web she caught a juicy fly.

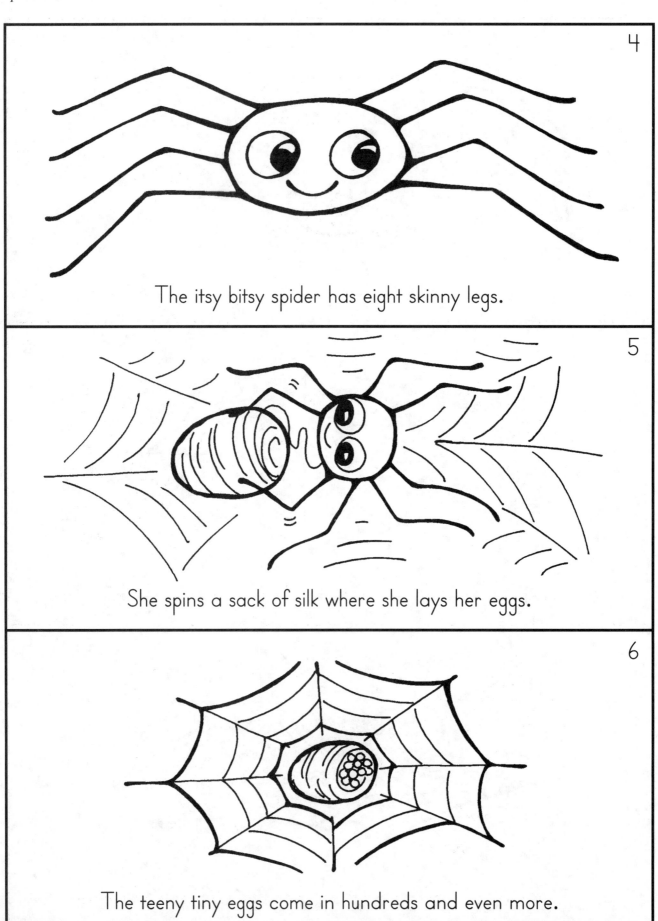

4

The itsy bitsy spider has eight skinny legs.

5

She spins a sack of silk where she lays her eggs.

6

The teeny tiny eggs come in hundreds and even more.

7

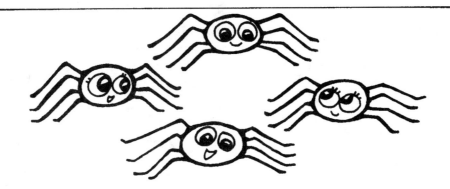

When the eggs begin to hatch, spiders crawl upon the floor.

8

Then the little spiders spin and sleep in their tiny webs.

9

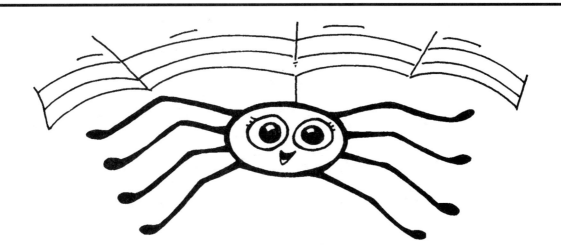

So this story just goes on and on since the spinning never ends.

1

Our Solar System

(tune: "Do You Know the Muffin Man?")

This book belongs to:

_____

2

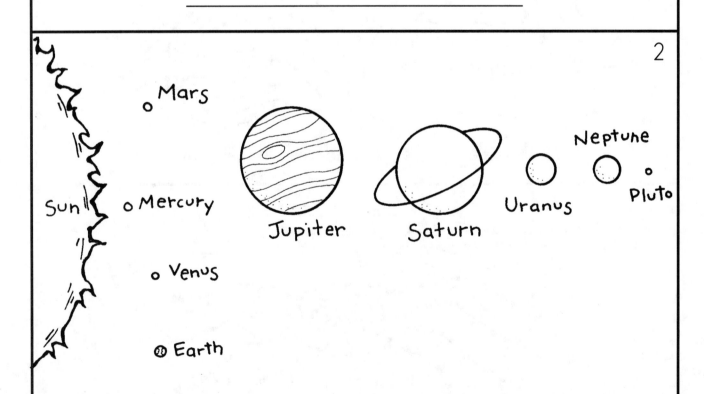

o Mars

Sun   o Mercury

Jupiter   Saturn   Uranus   Neptune   o Pluto

o Venus

⊕ Earth

There are nine planets in our solar system, solar system, solar system.

There are nine planets in our solar system, orbiting around the sun.

3

Our shining sun is the closest star, the closest star, the closest star.

Our shining sun is the closest star that keeps us cozy and warm.

4

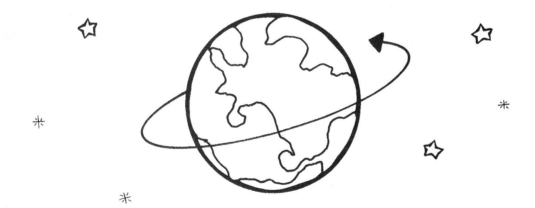

Our planet Earth spins round and round, round and round, round and round.

Our planet Earth spins round and round, one time every day.

5

When half the earth is in the day, in the day, in the day.

When half the earth is in the day, the other is in night.

6

It's a Fact!

When one half of the earth faces away from the sun, it is nighttime there, while it is daytime on the other side of the earth which is facing toward the sun. You can use a world globe and a flashlight to show this. Use the flashlight to represent the sun and hold it up to shine on the world globe. Slowly turn the globe but keep the flashlight still. What happens?

1

A Job for You!

(tune: "London Bridge")

This book belongs to:

_____

2

What is it you like to do,

Like to do, like to do?

What is it you like to do?

Oh, jobs, here we go!

3

Would you like to teach in school,

Teach in school, teach in school?

Would you like to teach in school?

Oh, jobs, here we go!

4

Is a computer fun for you,

Fun for you, fun for you?

Is a computer fun for you?

Oh, jobs, here we go!

5

Would you like to fly a plane,

Fly a plane, fly a plane?

Would you like to fly a plane?

Oh, jobs, here we go!

6

Or is it dogs you like to train,

Like to train, like to train?

Or is it dogs you like to train?

Oh, jobs, here we go!

7

Maybe you would like to cook,

Like to cook, like to cook.

Maybe you would like to cook.

Oh, jobs, here we go!

8

Can you write a storybook,

Storybook, storybook?

Can you write a storybook?

Oh, jobs, here we go!

9

Would you like to act on stage,

Act on stage, act on stage?

Would you like to act on stage?

Oh, jobs, here we go!

10

Perhaps you'd like to do a dance,

Do a dance, do a dance.

Perhaps you'd like to do a dance.

Oh, jobs, here we go!

11

Maybe sports are right for you,

Right for you, right for you.

Maybe sports are right for you.

Oh, jobs, here we go!

12

What is it you like to do,

Like to do, like to do?

What is it you like to do?

Oh, jobs, here we go!

1

My Grizzly Bear Book

(tune: "Daisy, Daisy")

This book belongs to:

_____

2

Grizzly, Grizzly, tell me all about you.

I am wondering about all the things you do.

3

I see you eating salmon.

At the river you stick your paw in.

4

Then you do eat a tasty treat
Of salmon just for you.

5

Grizzly, Grizzly, tell me more about you.

What else, Grizzly, do you like to do?

6

I see you raising bear cubs.

Do you wash them in a bathtub?

7

No! You stay clean in a mountain stream,
And your babies play there, too!

8

Here are more grizzly bear facts for you to read:

- Grizzly bears can grow up to eight feet tall and weigh 800 pounds.

- Grizzly cubs weigh one-half to one pound at birth and are born with their eyes closed and no fur. After two months they come out of the den. They live with their mother for one to two years.

- The life expectancy of a grizzly bear in the wild is fifteen to thirty years, but there are no more grizzlies living in the wild in California.

- Grizzly bears eat fish, meat, berries, plants, seeds, and more.

- The grizzly bear is the symbol on the California state flag.

9

Draw a picture of one of the grizzly bear facts.

1

My Summertime Book

(chant: "The Gingerbread Boy")

This book belongs to:

_____

2

Run, run as fast as you can

To keep yourself cool by the spinning fan.

3

Swim, swim in the swimming pool.

Swimming helps to keep you cool!

4

Climb, climb a mountain or tree.

Just be careful of the summertime bee!

5

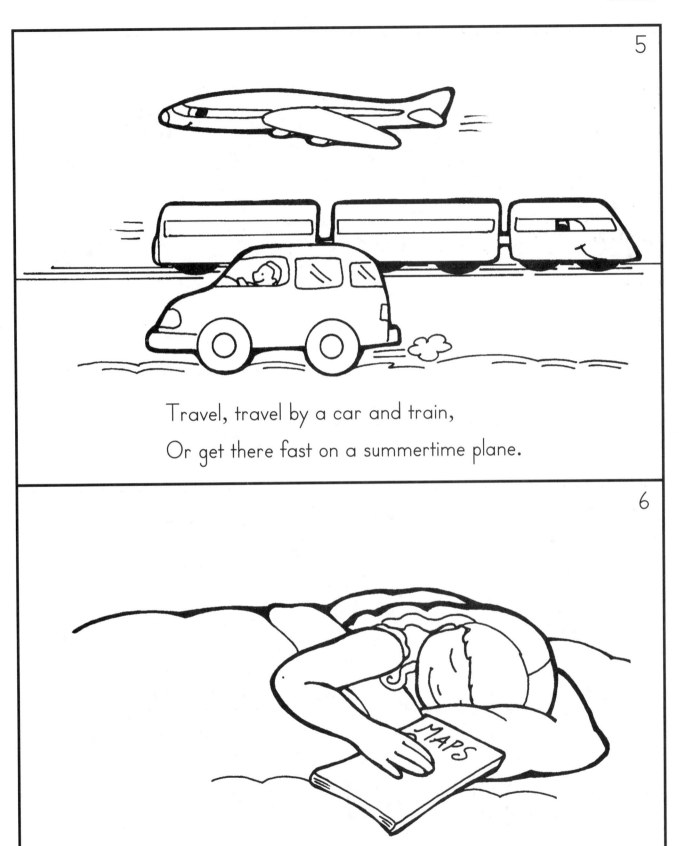

Travel, travel by a car and train,

Or get there fast on a summertime plane.

6

Read, read a good book or map,

But do not forget your summertime nap!

Summer Seashells

(tune: "The Twelve Days of Christmas")

This book belongs to:

_____

1

2

On the 1st day of summer my beach dog found for me
A conch shell by the blue sea.

3

On the 2nd day of summer my beach dog found for me
2 limpet shells and a conch shell by the blue sea.

4

On the 3rd day of summer my beach dog found for me

3 sundial shells and a conch shell by the blue sea.

5

On the 4th day of summer my beach dog found for me

4 cowrie shells and a conch shell by the blue sea.

6

On the 5th day of summer my beach dog found for me

5 horned shells and a conch shell by the blue sea!

On the 6th day of summer my beach dog found for me

6 scallop shells and a conch shell by the blue sea.

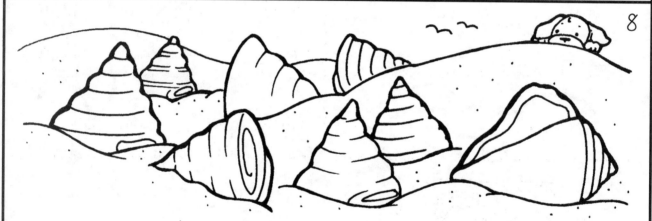

On the 7th day of summer my beach dog found for me

7 top shells and a conch shell by the blue sea.

On the 8th day of summer my beach dog found that he

Was so tired he fell asleep by the blue sea!

1

Turtle, Turtle

(tune: "Twinkle, Twinkle, Little Star")

This book belongs to:

_____

2

Turtle, turtle, swimming free,

3

You'll never be a pet for me.

4

Turtle, turtle, swimming to reach

5

The place you were born on a sandy beach.

6

Turtle, turtle, burying your eggs,

7

Using your flippers instead of legs.

8

Turtle, turtle, swimming free,

9

You're 100 pounds and bigger than me.

10

Turtle, turtle, with flippers so strong,

11

When grown up you're three feet long.

12

Turtle, turtle, swimming alone,

You like the ocean for your home.

1

Taking Care of Me, Your Puppy

(tune: "Take Me Out to the Ball Game")

This book belongs to:

_____

2

Take me out to the green park, take me out for a walk.

3

Buy me some dog food and tasty bones.

54

4

Please, don't leave me at home all alone.

5

I'll bark, bark, bark to protect you,

6

And never chew on your shoe!

7

For it's 1, 2, 3 hugs for me,

8

I'm your friend, true blue!

9

If I could have any pet in the world it would be a _____.

Here is a picture of my pet and me.

1

Johnny Appleseed

(tune: "This Old Man")

This book belongs to:

_____

2

This one man, he planted seeds.

He planted seeds that grew into trees.

3

With a knickknack paddywack, plant some apple seeds.

Then they'll grow into apple trees.

4

Soon there were apples to share,

Tasty apples everywhere.

With a knickknack paddywack, plant some apple seeds.

Then they'll grow into apple trees.

5

People called him Johnny Appleseed,

And they thanked him for his deed.

With a knickknack paddywack, plant some apple seeds.

Then they'll grow into apple trees.

6

Here are some tasty things made from apples:

apple pie

applesauce

apple dumplings

apple butter

caramel apples

Which is your favorite food made from apples?

1

I'm an Orange Pumpkin

(tune: "I'm a Little Teapot")

This book belongs to:

_____

2

I'm an orange pumpkin, round and fat,

But I didn't always look like that!

3

Before I turned orange, I was green and small,

Still in the shape of a little ball.

4

I grew from a flower on a vine.

My friends and I grew in a line.

5

The vine grew from a seed in
the ground,

Oval shaped and not too round.

6

The pumpkin seed needed water
and sun

To help it grow and have
some fun!

7

The sun did shine and the rain
did fall,

So, we began to grow, one
and all.

8

My life story, now you know,

All about the way I grow.

9

You can draw some faces on me.
Make them cute, funny, or scary!

10

My Cute Pumpkin

11

My Funny Pumpkin

12

My Scary Pumpkin

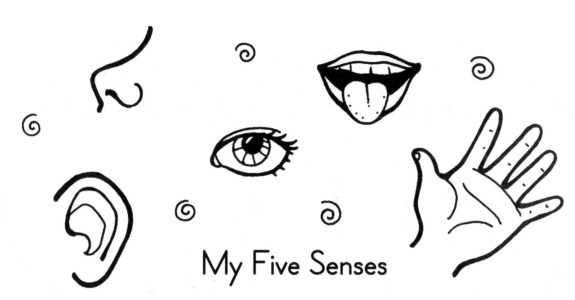

1

My Five Senses

(tune: "Row, Row, Row Your Boat:)

This book belongs to:

_____

2

Taste, taste, taste your food, using your taste buds.

Yummy, yummy, yummy, yummy, but never eat soap suds!

3

Hear, hear, hear your cat, hear your cat meow.

Meow, meow, meow, meow, better feed it now!

4

Touch, touch, touch the fur, touch the kitten's fur.

Quiet, quiet, quiet, quiet, listen to it purr.

5

Smell, smell, smell the cookies, smell the cookies bake.

Chewy, chewy, chewy, chewy, special treats to make.

6

See, see, see the stars, filling up the sky.

Twinkle, twinkle, twinkle, twinkle, one just flew right by!

1

I'm So Thankful

(tune: "Rockabye Baby")

This book belongs to:

_____

2

I am so thankful for stars and sky.

I am so thankful for clouds rolling by.

3

I am so thankful for food I eat.

4

I am so thankful for birds that tweet.

5

I am so thankful for plants and trees.

6

I am so thankful for rivers and seas.

7

I am so thankful for family.

8

I am so thankful just to be me!

9

Here are pictures of other things for which I am thankful.

1

In the Fall

(tune: "London Bridge Is Falling Down")

This book belongs to:

_____

2

Colorful leaves are falling down, falling down, falling down.

3

Colorful leaves are falling down onto the wet ground.

4

Pumpkins grow on a vine, on a vine, on a vine.

5

Pumpkins grow on a vine. I'll carve a face on mine.

6

We give thanks for tasty food, tasty food, tasty food.

We give thanks for tasty food. Fall tastes are very good!

1

Why Does It Snow?

(tune: "The Itsy Bitsy Spider")

This book belongs to:

_____

2

The dark cloud in the sky is very, very cold.

3

It's made of ice crystals that aren't very old.

4

Water drops stick to the crystals and freeze.

5

These are so very cold they could probably make you sneeze.

6

The crystals begin to grow bigger and bigger yet.

7

Until at last they're snowflakes, cold and wet.

8

The snowflakes fall so heavy from the sky.

9

When the wind begins to blow, it looks like they could fly!

10

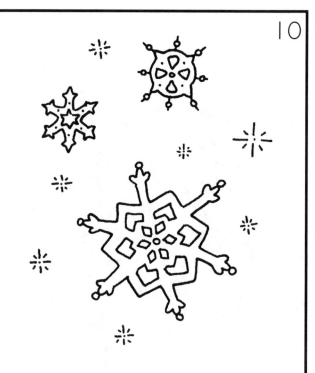

Every single snowflake looks different from the other.

11

If you don't believe me, ask your mother.

12

Now, to help remember, here's a review. All the pictures on this page have been placed here just for you!

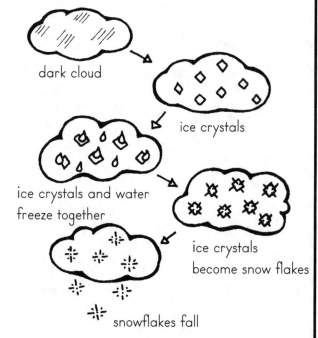

dark cloud

ice crystals

ice crystals and water freeze together

ice crystals become snow flakes

snowflakes fall

1

Winter

(tune: "Clementine")

This book belongs to:

_____

2

It is winter, it is winter, it is winter when it snows.

3

It is winter when the north wind starts to blow upon my nose.

4

It is winter, it is winter, it is wintertime right now.

5

If you don't know how to snow board, I would love to show you how.

6

It is winter, it is winter, it is wintertime outside.

7

I am ready for adventure on a super fast sled ride!

8

It is winter, it is winter, it is wintertime today!

9

Let's hurry and dress warmly so Mom will let us out to play.

10

It is winter, it is winter, it is winter and I'm cold.

11

I think I'll stay here by the fire until I've grown very old!

What do you like to do in the winter? Draw your favorite winter activity here.

12

Bibliography

This is a bibliography of suggested additional reading by month and topic.

January

Esbensen, Barbara Juster. ***Baby Whales Drink Milk.*** *(Let's Read and Find Out Science, Stage 1).* HarperCollins, 1994.

Gunzi, Christiane. ***Look Closer: Tide Pool.*** DK Publishing, 1998.

February

Adler, David A. ***A Picture Book of Abraham Lincoln.*** Holiday House, 1990.

Adler, David A. ***A Picture Book of George Washington.*** Holiday House, 1990.

Roop, Connie. ***Let's Celebrate Valentine's Day***. Horn Book, 1999.

March

Bingham, Caroline. ***Big Book of Things That Go.*** DK Publishing, 1994.

Dodson, Peter. ***An Alphabet of Dinosaurs.*** Scholastic Trade, 1995.

April

Heller, Ruth. ***Chickens Aren't the Only Ones.*** Paper Star, 1999.

Fowler, Alan. ***How Do You Know It's Spring?*** Children's Press, 1991.

May

Hickman, Pamela. ***A New Butterfly: My First Look at Metamorphosis.*** Kids Can Press, 1997.

Parsons, Alexandra. ***Amazing Spiders.*** Alfred Knopf, 1990.

June

Becklake, Sue. ***All About Space*** *(Scholastic First Encyclopedia).* Scholastic Trade, 1999.

Rockwell, Anne F. ***Career Day.*** HarperCollins, 2000.

July

Crewe, Sabrina. ***The Bear*** *(Life Cycles).* Raintree/Steck Vaughn, 1997.

Fowler, Allan. ***How Do You Know It's Summer?*** *(Rookie Read About Science).* Children's Press, 1992.

August

Cain, Sheridan. ***Little Turtle and the Song of the Sea.*** Crocodile Books, 2000.

Morris, Solene. ***The Concise Illustrated Book of Sea Shells.*** Gallery Books, 1990.

Bibliography (cont.)

September

Handelman, Dorothy. *The Best Pet Yet (Real Kids Reader, Level 2).* Millbrook Press Trade, 1998.

Warrick, Karen Clemens. *John Chapman: The Legendary Johnny Appleseed.* Enslow Publishing, 2001.

October

Burckhardt, Ann L. *Pumpkins (Early Reader Science: Foods).* Bridgestone Books, 1996.

Hewitt, Sally. *The Five Senses (It's Science).* Children's Press, 1999.

November

Hirschi, Thomas Mangelsen. *Fall.* Cobblehill, 1991.

Rader, Laura. *A Child's Story of Thanksgiving.* Ideals Children's Books, 1998.

December

Jordan, Sara. *Celebrate Seasons (book and cassette).* Sara Jordan Publishing, 1999.

Arvetis, Chris and Carole Palmer. *Why Does It Snow?* Field Productions, 1986.

Additional Resources:

Burda, Jan. *Year Round Units for Early Childhood.* Teacher Created Materials, 2000.

Rice, Dona Herweck, *et.al. Write Time for Kids: Write Start.* Teacher Created Materials, 2001.